# Your Guide to Healthy Hair

Part One: Your Hair Is Your Glory Series

## Judy S. Carasco

BK Royston Publishing
P. O. Box 4321
Jeffersonville, IN 47131
502-802-5385
http://www.bkroystonpublishing.com
bkroystonpublishing@gmail.com

© Copyright – 2017

All Rights Reserved. No part of this book may be reproduced, stored in a retrieval system, or transmitted by any means without the written permission of the author.

Cover Design: Bill Lacy Designs

Cover Photo Credit: Paul Alexis

ISBN-10: 1-94611116-3

ISBN-13: 978-1-94611116-6

Printed in the United States of America

# Acknowledgement

TO God My Creator:

Thank you for birthing in me the gift of hair and a desire to help others achieve their best hair yet.

To My Husband Giovanni & Son Malachi

Thank you for your support and for cheering me on with the dreams that have been birthed into me! Love you with everything in me! This is for you both!

To My Mommy & Daddy

Thank you for your sacrifice and endless love for me. I am who I am today because of you.

To My Eight Sisters:

Genie, Ismaelle, Idette, Mary, Ashley, Ariel, Natalie, and Christina

Thank you for being my first clients, and for volunteering your hair, skin, nails and body in order for me to grow in my craft. I am blessed to have you all as sisters. Thank you for praying for me, and for challenging me to do better!

To my Four Brothers:

Apolos, Alexander, Paul & Ruben

Thank you for being volunteers while I experimented and grew in the beauty business. I hope this ignites a fire into your soul! Let's make it happen!

To My Spiritual Sisters:

Bibiane & Ruthie! Your matchless support is astonishing! I love you for your guidance and wisdom. Thank you for sticking by my side all these years!

# Table of Contents

Acknowledgements
Introduction & Humble Beginnings

| | |
|---|---|
| **Chapter One: Why Do We Love Hair?** | 1 |
| **Chapter Two: To those Who Change Lives Everyday** | 5 |
| **Chapter Three: A Tragedy Turned into Joy** | 11 |
| **Chapter Four: How Hair Works** | 17 |
| **Chapter Five: Diet, Exercise and a Rose Bush!** | 23 |
| **Chapter Six: Compliments and Don't do it!** | 29 |
| **Chapter Seven: How to choose your Stylist and Salon** | 33 |
| About the Author | 43 |

# Introduction

Hello Ladies!

This has been a project that was once a dream and now is physical reminder of how God will give you a dream. Now it's up to you to run with it, put in the work, and trust in Him that all things are working for your good. When a dream becomes a reality, it is a great feeling. I absolutely love what I do! The feeling that I get when a guest walks through the door one way and leaves totally transformed is unexplainable. I have been in the industry professionally for a decade, and I can say that I have seen, heard and experienced many salon scenarios thus far. I hope to be in this industry for many more decades to come and continue to bless many more lives. So why did I write this book? This book is written in order to inspire you. It is for women who have the desire for healthier hair and life style over all. I wanted to take you on this journey in order to encourage you to make better choices and be determined to care for your hair.

Our hair is our Crown; each strand radiates with beauty and grace especially when it's styled. Often times we don't feel beautiful, especially when we are going through life's challenges. Hormonal changes, poor eating habits and lack of exercise are all factors that we must consider. Our hair is a direct reflection of what's going into our bodies. Medications and toxins from chemically enhanced foods all have a negative effect on our hair. In order to maintain healthy hair there are several things we must do and stop doing.

I consider myself a healthy hair stylist, because I aim to treat and maintain balance in my client's hair. I hope to aspire each of you reading this series to want to do better, and to seek a professional stylist that can help you get there. I want to shed some light on the many problems that we as women face especially in the beauty industry. I aim to be transparent, and through transparency share my heart with you. I will also share tips and techniques that are great for styling different hair types in this series. In the few years that I've been in the industry, I've learned many things that I will share with you to educate you on caring for your hair more efficiently.

I want to be honest in my past struggles as a stylist. At one point in my life, I was an unprofessional stylist that just "did" hair. Without having the proper person to guide me and to steer me in the right direction, I was driving 200 miles per hour in the wrong direction! I had to experience unprofessionalism in order to recondition myself from continuing to do hair and the business of beauty the wrong way. It says in Romans 12:2, "but be transformed by the renewal of your mind, that you may prove what is that good and acceptable and perfect will of God." (New King James Bible). I knew God had a plan for me; I just needed to pay attention to the signs He was giving to me. That's exactly what had to happen to me; a changed mind! Changed surroundings, changed thinking and a desire to do better and be better. I started attending hair seminars and hair shows. I desired to master my craft and become an expert. I became a part of a mentorship group of stylist who want to do better.

Once I gave birth to my son Malachi, the process that I was going through in my mind was ignited by the desire to do better for him and my husband. They are my motivation, and why I do what I do. They encourage me and push me to be a better wife, mother, sister, friend, auntie, and daughter of the King!

So I took a step of faith, and now here I am writing this series as an aid in helping women all over the world understand their crown and how to maintain it! I desire and strive to do everything in excellence. Yes sometimes I do fall short, but the great thing about falling is that you can always get right back up! Nothing was handed to me and I worked very hard to be where I am today. I came from being unable to comprehend the business of beauty, to launching a beauty brand.

I had to change my mindset, surroundings and my circle of influencers. I had to make the decision to learn new techniques even when it seemed that I would never understand. I had to keep pushing even when I was discouraged and felt like giving up. I had to keep praying and receive the hope and encouragement that the Lord sent my way. This growing period in my life has shaped me into becoming a better person and stylist all together. The lessons I have learned so far has given me hope in the gifts that the Lord has given me. And with that I am just getting started! The best is yet to come, and I'm excited to see God's plan for my life develop and come into fruition! I'm excited about helping you look and feel your best.

# Humble Beginnings

Everyone has a story of how they began in the beauty industry; mine is quite unique. My eight sisters were my first clients, and are till this day. Yes, I said eight! I started off in the beauty industry by doing manicures and pedicures at home for my family and friends. I had friends and family over every weekend, and I would practice until I grew in the skill of nail artistry. I began to build my nail kit: received nail polish, gems stones, acetone and various supplies from my 'clients'. I was encouraged by this. I am forever grateful to those who have contributed in shaping my passion for the industry. I had always loved doing nails and nail art on my sisters, but I wanted to do more and get deeper into this industry. During the weekends as I got better at my craft, I would bring my nail kit to church and just do nails after choir rehearsal on my friends. One day, I decided to begin charging for the services hoping to make a few dollars to support my dream. At the churches fundraisers, everyone knew 'Judy would bring her nail kit'. I remember people would secretly come to me and say: "Can I be your first appointment, so that no one takes my ideas for the designs that I want on my nails?"

It was a full day of manicures, pedicures, and I would have young and old men and women all day. At the fundraisers, people would fuss at each other as to who goes first since I didn't have a real appointment book at the time. If someone wanted something done that day, they knew they just better hop right into the chair once I finished with someone. It was amusing seeing how some would argue and shove each other to sit down first. It was like watching a few friends play musical chairs, and once the music stops everyone is scrambling to find a seat. I remember the smile on the faces of the people once I finished; how they would grin from ear to ear, because I gave them a new style on their nails or it was shiny and perfectly polished. It was then that I realized that I had a natural talent for making people feel better about themselves. So, I decided to answer the call to join the beauty industry.

Fast forward a few years later, I went to nail tech school for a three-month period and became a licensed nail tech in the state of Florida. After about a year, my hair stylist at the time was a dear friend named Tabitha. She is one of the sweetest and genuine persons on the face of Gods earth. Tabitha would encourage me to go to cosmetology school and get my license to do hair. I loved watching her style and care for her client's hair. It gave me a longing to do the same, and the rest is history! So, Tabitha thank you so much for planting that seed in me! May Yawh continue to shine His face upon you and grant you the desires of your heart!

Now, let's begin the journey and make your hair your glory!

"Working with Judy Carasco, also known as P31Artistry has been an amazing experience! I've had the pleasure of partaking in this journey for over 15 years and I can truly say that passion and love is the source of the art that is produced with P31. From the moment you sit in a chair you not only receive great service and results you receive knowledge and understanding of how to make and keep your hair strong and healthy! I thank Judy and the P31 team for making me look and feel beautiful and making My Hair My Glory!

~With Love and Fabulous Hair, Mariama A."

# Chapter One

## Why Do We Love Hair?

Let's discuss hair. Why do we care for it? Why does it have the ability to change our mood, or self-esteem? Well, it's a part of us that we cherish. Whether we relax, color or leave it natural, we care for it. Not just because it's a part of our bodies, but because it's our crown. When styled, it enhances our look. A new style makes us feel alive! This all natural accessory can really make each of us feel great about ourselves, and it can actually make or break our mood. Have you ever had a bad hair day? How did you feel when your lovely strands decided to rebel and go against what you had in mind for a style? What about when you style your hair only to walk outside and it turns into a frizz ball that looks like static attacked your strands. I'm sure it was frustrating to stand in front of your mirror only to be disappointed at the outcome; especially on a day when you are already running late.

Now, let's think happy thoughts. Think about a bride on the day of her wedding day. She is feeling glamorous; like a queen. The look is not complete without hair and make-up. When she is coming down the aisle in all her glory, everyone notices everything about her. Everything on her has to be on point, especially her hair. She is beautiful; hopefully it is one of the best days of her life. Though she is all dolled up from head to toe, what really completes the look is her hair. Once that tiara, veil, or head piece is placed upon her strand, it elevates her confidence and overall look. Oh, and of course that's when the tears begin to flow. She feels so beautiful. If you were ever a bride, let's reminisce back to your wedding day. If you loved your hair, what made you love it? Was it the loose or tight curls, twisted and tousled strands, the Dutch braid or the sleek and sophisticated bun that made you feel gorgeous?

However you wore it that day, I'm sure your hair was impactful to your mood and overall appearance. After all, your hair is your glory! It is the crown of which we pride ourselves as women. Our faces radiates with beauty when our hair is freshly styled and in place. It can change our attitude; make us feel even more beautiful when it is well managed. Anyone can obtain healthy, hydrated full of body tresses; rather you wear it curly or straight, relaxed or natural or even color treated. How is this possible you ask? Well keep reading, and I will help you discover the steps.

"I have been a client of Mrs. Judy since 2009. She does an incredible job! Judy doesn't just care about the way your hair looks, but she also cares about the health status of your hair. Most stylists only focus on the beauty aspect of the hair. Judy goes beyond this. She not only focuses on making your hair look amazing, but also the mechanics of your hair. She is extremely competent and passionate about hair. When I get my hair done by her, I not only feel beautiful, I look beautiful and I get non- stop compliments. Overall service rating= INCREDIBLE!

-Primose Lataillade

# Chapter Two

## To Those Who Change Lives Everyday

Alright! Now let's get right to it. To the stylist reading this book, I say: Kudos to you for your dedication to this industry, and to continuing to grow as an expert in this business. I want to encourage all those who chose to change lives every day through touching hair. We are a vital part of society that too often is not treated as a profession. Why? Well first and foremost, are we treating our career of choice as a hobby or profession? Society has lost respect in most arenas of the beauty industry due to the lack of professionals in it. What was once a pillar in our neighborhoods, has turned into a dreaded place of disorder. I'm not bashing any stylist, just wanting to shine a light on the basics that we tend to forget once we're behind the chair all day. Over time, these habits become a stagnant routine. This was once who I was. Now that I know better, I chose to do better. In actuality, we can do better once we know better. Here are a few things I want to share with my fellow stylist.

**First Lesson**: Pay attention to body language! If we pay attention, we can always tell when someone is going through a rough patch. You see, body language is so important. Our bodies are always speaking to us as well as others around us. Sometimes we can miss opportunities to cater to our guest, love on each other or just listen to what others have to share. For this very reason, many if not most women see the time in a salon as an escape away from all the chaos. It's a valuable time for each guest which may be the only piece of serenity they may have in their lives. When I see a guest come in with her shoulders slightly drooped over with the weight of the world on them or dragging her feet, it could be a sign that she may be going through a storm, a drought or dry season. So as a stylist, my job is to create an atmosphere where she's coming to be made over, relax and leave the cares of the world behind her. So, paying attention to our guest's body language is so important.

**Lesson Two**: Everyone's time is valuable!

When a stylist is with a guest, it's not time to answer our phones with our necks bent over holding it with our shoulders. (That's very uncomfortable by the way!) It's not the time for inappropriate conversations. Our guest comes to us in order to relax. Time is one of the many things that once it's gone we can't get more of. A guest experience is influenced by the amount of time they are in the salon, especially the amount of time spent waiting for their stylist. So, it is crucial to deliver to their experience. Here's an example of how a guest experience should go. You walk into the salon and you are greeted by the receptionist with a smile. She offers you a beverage and checks you in. Upon your arrival, your stylist is notified of your presence. She comes over to greet you as well as extending her hand in a polite gesture.

You are then escorted back to the styling chair where the proper inquiries are asked. After a consultation, you both head over to the shampoo bowl. This great vessel has been identified as an emblem of rest, relaxation and relief. The five to ten minutes at the shampoo bowl is crucial to all guest, so please aim to make it count.

As you proceed to style her hair, converse about life and the dreams you have. We can cry sometimes together. Laughter can be heard a mile away. Most importantly, hair education is essential part of the service. Finally, the service is complete when I spin my guest around for the big reveal! Now is the moment of truth. My guest looks into the mirror and sees her new self; while I'm saying to myself, "Wow, Judy girl you did that!" As she cracks a smile, touches her hair and says: "Oh my goodness, I love it!" I can't help but jump for joy on the inside! The icing on the cake is when my guest has gotten teary eyed at the sight of their hair.

This is one of the many encounters that I have had in the salon. I have serviced many guests, and along the way some have become more than a guest. They are a part of the family. You see, there's a bond that forms between a stylist and their guest. There's a connection that develops the moment the guest is greeted as they enter into the safe haven of the salon. The delicate touch during a shampoo service, ambiance of the salon and the smells of the professional products are all significant factors that create a lasting recollection for each person.

Lastly, I bet you can remember the very first time you've walked through a salon's doors. What did it look like? What did it smell like? Do you remember details of that experience and how you were treated during the service? If you're thinking: 'Why the big deal about ambience and details, I just need to make my money? Whether you have guest as an executive of a fortune five hundred company, a stay at home mom, a florist, deli manager or even a first lady of the local church, the salon is a home away from home for a lot of women. So what am I trying to say? Are your stations clean and spotless? Are the floors free of hair and debris? Can clients see themselves through the mirrors at your stations? Are they layered with hair spray and dust? Clean space is a key component to creating the prefect atmosphere for your guests. Everyone deserves our undivided attention. So are we gossiping with the next stylist or making our guest our number one priority? We are in this industry not because it something to do, but because we LOVE changing lives one strand at a time! Keep in mind we are not magicians; we create and deliver services that will change some one's life!

*" I have been fortunate to have found Judy. Transitioning to natural hair has had it's challenges and Judy has handheld it with ease. It's great having a seat in Judy's chair knowing that the finished product will always be above my expectations!"- Bianca Issacs*

# Chapter Three

## A Tragedy Turned Into Joy

As I stated before, I have been a stylist for nearly ten years professionally. I have had the opportunity to touch many lives, many of whom I will never forget. I always try to remember that some people that come into my life are here for a season. They are sent by the Lord to teach me, assist me, help me, counsel me and be the friend that I need in that particular moment and vice versa. With that being said, I must tell you about my lovely guest Anita. Anita represents a vast amount of women in the United States and abroad that have tried to care for their hair the best way they can. Anita suffers from what I call 'LKS', or the lack of knowledge syndrome. What I mean by this is, that most women like Anita have little to no knowledge when it comes to caring for their hair. Some of the culprits of this saddening situation are the excessive use of uncontrollable temperature of heat tools and improper installation of extensions. The lack of proper care has caused a tremendous amounts of damage to the hair fibers. The over use of chemicals on the hair has caused an epidemic. In addition to this, there's the lack of education from professional stylist. The overwhelming DIY video tutorials on YouTube have contributed to the crisis of unhealthy hair as well. Now back to Anita……

Anita walks in with a baseball cap on her head; hair pulled back into a ponytail. Her countenance has fallen. Looking at her as she walks through the doors, I wondered what her hair story was, and what the journey been like for her so far. I walked over to greet Anita and offer her a beverage. I ask her how's she's doing and what is she trying to accomplish, as she plops herself into my styling chair. Anita lets out a big sigh and says: "Huh, I'm so tired of my hair; I don't know what else I can do to it. I just can't deal with it anymore, so do whatever is necessary!" I ask "Anita, how do you feel about your hair?" To this she replies, "I just want healthy hair. I want to touch my real hair and not have to hide it anymore with wigs and extensions, because I'm so embarrassed. I just want you to make me feel and look whole again, so you can do whatever you want!" She proceeds to remove the baseball cap. Now for the big reveal!

I'm actually not surprised at what I see. Anita's hair was so broken in most areas due to the excessive use of extensions which were installed improperly. It is also evident that her hair is thirsty due to lack of hydration and negligence. As a stylist, I think to myself that this is just a sad situation. It's going to be a long day, and I'm glad I had a big lunch! I proceed to consult with Anita about her hair history, and I discover her hair care regime is nonexistent. She has it braided every two months, and she relaxes her hair herself once the braids are removed. Anita admits to me in one of the most painful statements a client can utter to a stylist, "Honey, I just go the beauty supply and grab the 'super' strength of whatever perm is on sale!"

"Whoa!" When I heard those words, my right eye begins to twitch! So I ask her, "Why she applies super strength of relaxer to her hair?"

I could see clearly that she clearly has a texture that really needs mild. "Well, I thought you can just put anyone of those in your hair as long as the hair is laid and smooth down right?"

To that I replied, "No ma'am! Relaxers are a chemical that should most definitely be applied by a professional stylist."

"Secondly, the hair has to be examined by doing an elasticity test which will determine what strength the hair has. Also the texture must be tested to ensure that the correct strength of relaxer is being used for the type of hair that you have. If the hair is not examined properly and any strength of relaxer is applied to the hair, it will be a recipe for disaster!" The look on Anita's face tells me that she has never heard this information before. I sense that she wants to learn more and begin a healthy hair journey that would give her the best hair she has ever had.

You see Anita, a majority of women have been going to the drug store for hair care products such as relaxers without the proper education of how they should be used and applied. The hair on Anita's head has been thinned out and over processed by default. Anita admits to applying her relaxer at home in the bathroom and leaving it in until it 'burns'! "Until it Burns!" I reply in amazement that her hair hasn't all disintegrated from the over processing that has occurred. "I tried doing it myself in order to save money. But I have destroyed my hair, and I need your help! I used to have hair that was full of body, thick and luscious. Now I am so embarrassed that I wear this cap, wigs or scarves in order for me to hide it and feel normal," expressed Anita.

I ask Anita the same questions that I started asking my entire guests: What would it mean to you to have healthy hair? How would it change your life?" With teary eyes, she sighs and says: "It would give me confidence in myself again. I would be able to look into a mirror and love what I see. I'm not comparing myself with celebrities or other women whom I have come to know. I just want to look like me with healthy hair. I am willing to do something different."

Listening to the desperation in her voice had me thinking: "If only every woman would be willing to do something different, learn new ways to care for their hair and together with their stylist create a regime that would give them their best hair yet.' This really had my mind going a million miles a minute! You see, just like Anita. It can even be you who's reading this book right now. You see, we are all the same. And as women we want to look our best. Regardless of financial status, ethnicity, relaxed or natural. The question is: Are we willing to change by renewing our minds, and learn some new techniques that are beneficial to the health of our hair and whole being. When our hair is freshly styled and laid in place, we radiate with an inner beauty that is incomparable. It can change our mood, making us feel as if we are on top of the world! It makes our hearts smile. So, we must do a better job of taking care of our tresses. Whether you wear it curly, straight, relaxed, natural or even color treated. Many women reading this book would love tips and tricks on hair care and maintenance. This is the purpose of this book. I encourage you to keep reading, and you'll discover the steps and hopefully create a regiment that will help you get there.

*"It's amazing how different we feel when our hair is done by someone we completely trust; especially, when it's done in a fresh new style that we absolutely love. As women, this makes us feel ready to step out into a crowd with confidence, do a hair toss and conquer the world! That is how Judy's incredible work makes me feel. She is extremely talented." – Rachel Isaacs*

## Chapter Four

### How Hair Works

Most women can obtain hair that is healthy, hydrated and full of body. The thought of having the hair you've always wanted can be a dream come true. Yet the question you must ask yourself is: Are you willing to implement new techniques, and change bad habits? 1 Corinthians 11:15 says: "If a woman have long hair, it is a glory for her!" Our hair is the crown in which we pride ourselves as women. The strands on our heads do not necessarily have to be long and flowing. It can be a tight coil, wavy like the oceans tides or straight as a hair pin. But however we choose to wear it, we must realize that our hair is our crown! So wear it well girls. There is absolutely no other feeling like a makeover. Whenever your hair is done and you put on your favorite outfit; you're out feeling like a million dollars. You know exactly what I am talking about, because we have all been there before.

Cherishing your strands can change our mood and bring a boost of self-confidence to women. That's exactly why you won't take a crown that radiates with beautiful jewels and glistens like the golden sun and mistreat it. It wouldn't be placed on the floor, or throw in a drawer collecting dust. Instead, we would have that crown on a soft pillow store in a glass case that is unbreakable. It would be on display for all to see it under security. The same goes for our hair ladies. Caring for our hair starts right now. We are losing our hair by the fistful due to improper care and misuse of commercial hair and chemicals. If our hair is so precious, then why are we tearing it apart with our poor upkeep and bad habits? These are some of the reasons why so many women are losing the glory that they carry.

Before we go any further, it's important to know what hair is. Our hair is comprised of 22 Amino Acids, which forms a bond and then they become proteins. These proteins are necessary for the building and repairing of tissues. Keratin is a protein that forms our hair; it is also made of 19 of the 22 amino acids. Our hair is made up of 97% keratin and 3% trace minerals. Amino acids form chains that are compounds of carbon; sulfur which are solids and three gases: hydrogen, nitrogen and oxygen.

These elements are the basic substances that make up our hair. Hair is made of proteins that are bonded together like chains which form our hair!

With that being said it is a tedious journey in order for hair to be formed on our heads. So why not uphold it and have your best hair? Again, our hairs are boosted by what nutrients we feed our bodies and how we care for our strands. Let's take it a step further. There are three stages of hair growth. And if you're hearing this for the first time, let me explain.

Three stages of hair growth

First and foremost our hair growth and health is dependent upon many factors. But first let us discuss the stages that make up the growing process of hair.

1. ANAGEN STAGE: is the active growing stage of hair. According to pivot point international 2000, 'on average 90 percent of a person's hair is in this stage which lasts from two to six years.' This means that during this time hair color is darker and fuller due to the growth of the hair. Hair on average grows ½ an inch per month. ( Source: salon fundamentals by pivot point International Inc. 2000 page 183)

2. CATAGEN STAGE is the second stage, and it's a transitional stage where the hair stops growing for a few weeks. This is the stage where most of us

feel like our hair is 'not growing.' And the truth is, that our hair is at a standstill and is preparing its self for the last and final stage.

**3. TELOGEN STAGE:** this final stage is most women's nightmare! It's where the hair bulb is no longer rooted. It's at this very stage that the hair falls out and sheds. Three to four months is the length of time that this stage lasts on average. It sounds terrifying doesn't it? But don't worry, the hair is preparing itself to begin again. Hair is rejuvenated and recharged over and over again. It is important to understand these cycles. Because as I mentioned before, most women are freaking out that they are going bald. Yet in actuality, the hair is just preparing its self for the next set of strands.

Remember the many factors that can affect hair growth and health that I mentioned before? Well, some of the culprits that can affect hair are: medications, diseases, poor diet, genetics and lack of exercise. The environment can change our hair within a matter of seconds. We've all been there where we style our hair and as soon as we step outside the humidity attacks. And before you know it, we have a frizz ball called hair! It's important that we use professional products such as Design Essentials Honey Crème Moisture Retention Shampoo and their Rosemary & Mint Stimulations Conditioner that adds moisture and gives out hair hydration as well.

# Chapter Five

## Diet, Exercise and a Rose Bush!

Do you look at your hair only hoping that it was: hydrated, full of body and radiant from roots to ends? Let's be honest we all do. And the good news is, your hair can be healthy, shiny and full of body. Whether you wear it curly, relaxed, natural or even color treated, your hair has to be treated weekly or biweekly in order to maintain its luster, body, moisture and strength. First things first! You have to become conscious of what you put into your body that will reflect on the hair strands. As a child, you were told to eat your vegetables and fruits and drink lots of water. Though you may have resisted, I hope that eventually as you grew into adulthood you grasped the benefits in doing so.

We've all heard the expression: 'you are what you eat,' and there is so much truth to this phrase. Diet and nutrition plays such an important role in our overall health and well-being. Ladies the truth is that if we don't have a balance diet that is rich in vitamins, water, fruits, vegetables, grains, proteins and good fats, our hair cannot be all that we hope it to be. Our hair is a reflection of what we eat. Have you ever thought of asking yourself these questions: What is my dream hair plan composed of, and how will I get there? What are my hair goals? How would drinking 8 glasses of water a day per day (Alkaline water would be the best choice for overall health) and eating at least four or multiple servings of fruits and vegetables each day change my hair and overall health? What am I doing to energize my body, and stay active? If these are not a part of your daily routine, I strongly encourage you to begin to eat healthier foods that are rich in vitamins, nutrients and drink more water. I cannot stress on the importance of these.

Your hair, skin, and nails are all linked together and their overall health is dependent on the foods we eat, vitamins we take, our exercise plan and beverages we consume every day. All these work in unity every day and are boosted by what nutrients we feed our bodies and how we care for our strands.

The best way I can explain this to you, is how I explain it to my guest at the salon. This is as simple as it gets: 'Hair is like a plant. Let's take a rose bush for example. The flowers stems and branches are similar to the structure of our hair strands. The roots are comparable to the hair bulb. There are several steps to care and nurture a rose bush. Step one, the bush must be planted in good fertile ground; also it must be watered daily in order to ensure hydration. Likewise, our bodies need hydration that comes from water. Not only to filter out the toxins in our hair, but in our skin and body as a whole.

Water is drawn up from the roots into the stems and branches giving life to the rose buds. Next, the fertilizers and supplements that are put into the soil regularly penetrates the plant in order to supply it with nutrients so it can be full of healthy luscious roses that radiates with beauty from root to flower petals! Let's not forget the sun that shines down to give the rose bush a boost each day. In the same way, our nutrition and vitamin supplements are vital parts of the feel, appearance and the overall health of our mane.

Lastly, the bush has to have a regiment for trims and cut backs of the branches in order for it to grow healthier and fuller as well. Now, this is the part that guests do not like! I can guess that when you see your stylist pull out their shears (you all call them hair scissors, but they are shears, lol), I can imagine that your heart starts racing about 50 miles per hour! Regular trims not only seals the ends of each strand, but it helps prevent further damage to hair that is soon to spilt and break from several factors. It is necessary ladies that your ends are sealed professionally between 8-10 weeks; depending on how your hair grows and the styling routine that you practice. You must trust your stylist and understand that they have your best interest in mind.

I hope this simplified hair health and growth for you. I like to use this analogy, because it helps guest to get a clearer picture of what is happening to their hair whenever I am servicing them by caring for their hair. The fibers on our head are very delicate, and we have to do better at caring for the hair that grows out of our scalp. If you are suffering from dry brittle hair that is life less it's more than likely that your hair is not receiving nourishment as it should.

If your diet is made up of fast foods, sodas, fried foods, sugars and unwholesome fats, it's not surprising that the hair strands are dull and crying out for help! Also, let's keep in mind that someone that is on heavy medications are probably struggling with shedding and parched hair as well; which can alter the growth and health of our hair as well. If this is you, increasing your water intake will help your body to pass the toxins and medications out of your body faster.

Seek the help of a Trichologist. A Trichologist is a professional that studies the science of hair and scalp. Together they will work with you towards your hair health and goals, whatever it may be. It will be a great partnership to begin a healthy hair regiment with a stylist or hairdresser that practices healthy hair on all levels of service in their salon. What I mean by this is, they are applying chemicals safely and properly. Precautions are in place to ensure the hair's integrity is not compromised. They are educating you about home maintenance and care for your hair in between salon visits.

Exercise helps to stimulate the blood circulation in our bodies and bring it all throughout the body. The scalp receives the oxygen and nutrients needed to promote healthy hair and scalp. Cardio exercise such as dancing, cycling, jump roping, running on a treadmill all are great ways to get our hearts pumping and to send oxygen rich blood to our scalp. Another way to promote hair growth, is by performing a scalp massage for at least 30 seconds a day! The blood flow and stimulation again will assist in hair growth and health. So ladies, let's get moving and active in order to activate hair growth!

# Chapter Six

## Compliments and Don't Do It!

In this chapter, I hope that you get an understanding of which styles are complimenting to your face shape and your overall look. The right style for your face does wonders. You can't imagine the change it makes to yourself esteem when you are wearing the best cut, style and overall look for your face shape. It's a common mistake that we make when we try the latest styles because it is the latest fad. There are styles that are really appealing, yet without the proper education, you just don't know that it doesn't fit your face shape. The style can be modified to fit your face frame. A word of advice: 'Every style is not for everybody.'

To begin, there are 7 common facial shapes. What are they? Glad you asked! Oval, Round, Square, Oblong or long, Pear, Diamond and Heart. Let's take a closer look at these lovely shapes. Oval:

is also known as the ideal face shape or the most versatile. Oval shapes can use strong styles such as a pixie cut or bobs; layering all create drama and gives you a better look. The second shape is Round. A round face looks great with short layered styles; wispy sides around the cheeks will give the face an appearance of being slimmer. You also want to avoid volume and curls especially at the sides since it will cause the face to appear wide. Round faces overall are better and balanced with asymmetrical cuts and styles since they change the angles of the face creating an illusion of length.

The Square face is next. It is structured with strong angles and has very dominated features. To soften this shape, you are better off with height or volume at the top of the head. You can also look your best by avoiding straight bangs and styles that stop at the jaw line.

Let's go over the Oblong or Long shape now. It is also known as the rectangle face shape and is in need of softness. Softness can be created by adding volume around the chin. Please avoid pixie cuts or straight hair, since this look makes the hair more masculine and the face even longer. Pear shapes have a narrow forehead and wider jaw line: therefore, its best to style this shape with volume above the jaw line. Likewise, hair should pass the jaw line in order to create a slimming effect. You should avoid styles that stop right at the jaw line, since it will create more width.

The sixth shape is the Diamond. Diamonds are a girl's best friend right?! Well, you may not have diamonds for jewels, but if you have a face shaped like one you can love your look even more after this lesson! As a natural diamond gets wider in the middle, so it is with your face. You'll find that the cheekbones are the widest part of your face thus, creating the result of this precious jewel. Here's the solution! Keeping the hair around the nape a little longer will balance the face and create a softer look adding fullness along the chin. But above the head, you want to be cautious of adding too much volume and height on top.

Lastly but certainly not least, let's discuss the matters of the Heart. The shape is like an upside down triangle. It can be soften with curls and added volume at the chin. Long layers are complementing as well. Please avoid cropped cuts that rest at the neck, because it will create a harsher look that should be avoided.

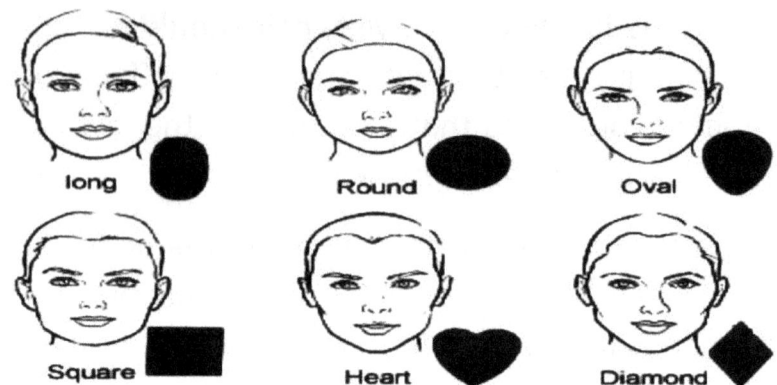

Did this help you get a better understanding of the right style for your face? I hope so. The difference the right style makes can be life changing. Now, let's move and discuss how you can choose the right stylist and salon for your patronage.

(PICTURESOURCE:BEAUTYANDFASHIONFREAKS.COM/WP-CONTENT/UPLOADS/2014/10/FACE-TYPES.JPG)

# Chapter Seven

## How to Choose Your Stylist and Salon

The relationship between a client and a stylist is one that quite often molds into friendship. What do I mean? Well, many women have confided several of their life's situations in their stylist. The relationship has flourished from a client and stylist relationship into something more. The cosmetology industry has evolved into an inspirational and safe haven for many clients. It has always been a place of shared thoughts, feelings and emotions. Clients and stylist have both received advice and encouragement on many levels.

So with that being said, I must address some issues that are happening now in this industry. For Starters, I am aware of the many consumers like you who are tired of spending their hard earned dollars at 'shops' that double and triple book their appointments. Not only are you frustrated and tired of it; well I'll be blunt, its rude and disrespectful to wait at the salon for five or six hours for just a roller set or relaxer. Your time and the time of each client are valuable and precious. Time is never given back, so spending your whole

Saturday at the 'shop' really is tragic. There, I said it! Many clients are sick and tired of waiting. And most of the time its poor planning and booking on our part as stylist, so on behalf of the entire beauty industry who desires for our guest to have a better experience at our salons, I apologize.

Woo! (wipes forehead). Now that I have that off my chest, there is absolutely no comparison to being serviced in a professionally ran salon. Imagine this! You have just moved into a new town, and you're in need of a haircut or style for the office Christmas party. So, like anyone else, would you ask coworkers for recommendations for a salon since you are new to the area? Maryann from accounting suggests her stylist Judy, and gives you the salons business card. So, you take the business card and call the salon. The phone rings a few times before it's answered. A polite smiling voice answers the phone. "Good afternoon, and thank you for calling Elegance Salon and Spa. How can I help you? You reply, "Oh Hi, my name is Bibiane Jones. I am new to this area, and I am in desperate need of a new stylist. Can you help me?"

The sweet young lady joyfully replies, "We sure can help you, can you tell me a little bit more of what services you need us to provide for you?

"Well, I was referred by Maryann Thomas, who is a client of your salon. And I would like an up do and a manicure for our office Christmas party next week Friday. Do you have anything available?" To that the receptionist replies, "We just have one appointment slot for Friday December 18$^{th}$ at 3:30 pm for a formal style and manicure, will that work for you Bibiane?" To your amazement there was an opening, so you reply quickly before the spot is taken. "That will work; I'm only working half a day and I have plenty of time to get my hair and nails done before the party. It's perfect!" "Well it sounds like you are excited about your appointment," replies the receptionist. Ms. Bibiane, your stylist will be Grace and your manicurist is Joanne. They both are highly recommended and experienced and will cater to your needs also. Our address is 555 Elegance Blvd; we are the white two story building with tropical flowers and a waterfall on your left. Now when you pull in, park on the Northwest side of the building for it is more accessible for our guests."

The receptionist proceeds to tell you the forms of payment the salon accept. The custom is for first time guests to arrive 15 minutes prior to their appointment time for a quick tour of the salon and spa. Bibiane is so intrigued by the first impression she's had with the receptionist that she cannot wait for Friday to get here and finally experience a professional the salon.

It's Friday December 18$^{th,}$ and Bibiane has been watching the clock all day anticipating her appointment! It's now 3 o'clock and Bibiane rushes out of the office and heads to 555 Elegance Blvd. Upon her arrival, she notices the tropical plants and the waterfall. The scenery is absolutely breath taking! Remembering to park on the northwest side of the building, Bibiane enters through the double doors of Elegance Salon and spa. Immediately, the receptionist greets her and offers a beverage. The tour begins. First on the salon floor, Bibiane notice all the stylists engaging with their guests and having a wonderful time with each other. There's a song of laughter, and the rustling sound of blow driers prepping and polishing the clients hair.

There are no loud televisions playing or unprofessional conversations going on. Bibiane thinks to herself 'This is impressive'. They move into the shampoo area, and Bibiane is taken away at the relaxing atmosphere there. Clients are reclined back into the sinks with their feet up. They are receiving scalp and hand massages while the treatments are on their hair. "I've never seen such a relaxing shampoo room before; I can't wait for my turn!" "Rightfully so," replies the receptionist. "Our entire staff is trained by our therapist in the massage department to give the Elegance signature scalp and hand massage to each of our guests."

Bibiane is shown where the restrooms are as well as the lockers for her valuables. On her way to the waiting area, she notices something that she's never seen before. There's a stylist and client laughing so hard with each other, and they both are shedding tears of joy. Their connection is mind boggling. It's genuine and there is not a line of clients waiting for their turn for the stylist who happened to triple booked her guest. Wow, I've been waiting for an experience like this. Bibiane thinks to herself and thinks back to the old 'shop' she used to go to; "Going in, there was a full day of waiting and waiting. There was no receptionist to greet me, and I sure was not offered a beverage upon my arrival."

She reminisces about being overlooked and underserved, but not anymore! Bibiane has finally found a salon she can call home. Her thoughts are interrupted by a gentle voice, "Excuse me, are you Bibiane?" The polite young stylist comes over to introduce herself. "Yes I am." replies Bibiane. "Hello, my name is Grace," as she extends her hands to shake Bibiane hands she says; "I'll be your stylist today." "It's a pleasure to meet you," replies Bibiane. "The pleasure is all mines. Let's head over to my station, so we can consult about your hair service today. We're going to be at the station to your right near the window."

As they make it to the window, Bibiane is enveloped by the peaceful atmosphere that has embraced her since the parking lot. 'I like this' she thinks to herself. "They are consistent, and they follow through". As the service goes on they have conversations about her hair, and the stylist gives her education about maintaining it at home in between salon visits. They didn't veer off to talk about the latest celebrity gossip; it was pure education and ways to get healthier hair! "I'm definitely not used to this," Bibiane told Grace. "I used to have to sit and get an ear full about who's dating who, and who's doing what from my old salon. I wasn't trying to hear all that! I just had a hard day at work, and I just wanted to relax and get pampered. But my stylist just didn't catch the clues, when I tried changing the subject. I thank you for keeping it professional Grace, I am truly blessed by your presence."

To that Grace reply, "That's what a salon and spa is supposed to be dear. It's a home away from home. Where women and men can escape their realities of work, home and school for a few minutes or hours. I never understood this until I began working here at Elegance Spa and Salon. It has changed my life and the way I serve my guests. You see Bibiane, I was once that uneducated stylist that would gossip about what celebrities are doing, and who their new beaus are. I didn't have time for showing my clients how to care for their hair in between visits. I was so booked and over booked that I had to rush through the day and get clients in and out. Honestly, I was just thinking about getting money and not about healthy hair."

I had enough! One day after I took a class on the business of beauty, it finally hit me that I was doing it wrong. When I felt over whelmed and burned out, I had to redirect myself and change the route that I was on. I am eternally grateful for salons such as this place that gives us continuing education and pushes us to be greater and better.

Grace had just about finished and it was time for the manicure. "Now, Bibiane you will be getting a manicure today by Joanne. She is an amazing Nail Tech, and you are in good hands. It was a pleasure serving you today, I hope to see you soon, and Joanne will escort you to the receptionist once your manicure is completed. After the deluxe and relaxing manicure, Bibiane is escorted to the receptionist by Joanne, and she thanks Joanne for her professionalism. She thinks to herself, 'This was just an unbelievable experience.' As she gets to the counter, the receptionist asks, "how was your experience today Bibiane?" To that Bibiane replies, "this was such an amazing experience for me, it was impeccable! My hair is gorgeous and the manicure was absolutely amazing just as Grace said it would be."

"I am glad you enjoyed your visit today Bibiane, so when would you like to return for another great experience?" asked the receptionist. Bibiane responds without hesitation, "Please rebook me for two weeks with Grace and Joanne please."

Bibiane pays for her services and heads out to her car, thinking "This was an amazing experience, and I can't imagine not coming to this place, or being in an atmosphere such as this. I'm ready for this Christmas party!"

Back to reality. How is your experience at the salon? Are you experiencing half of that which Bibiane has experienced? If, not you should think about what you deserve, and work hard for. Here are somethings to pay attention to when looking for a stylist or salon:

- Are they on time or always late?
- Are they over booking guests?
- Are you being educated about the products being used and why they are using it on your hair?
- Is the stylist interested in the health of your hair or the money?
- Are you getting suggestions about what your options are for your hair, when you want a certain style that wouldn't be healthy for your hair?

I hope this book has started a fire in your soul to want and desire healthier hair. My prayers are that more of you will become more aware of what is happening to your hair. And that you are willing to change your lifestyle for overall health and wellness. Having read this book, may it cause you to seek a professional salon to go to receive your hair services. If you haven't began to eat healthier for your well-being, then now is the time to do so. You are what you eat; so eat well, drink lots of water and exercise as much as possible. Ladies, may you be encouraged and strengthen to make better choices for 'Your Hair is Your Glory!'

I was one of Judy's first clients when she began her career as a stylist. My first experience with Judy was when she perform a relaxer in my hair. I absolutely loved how she brought so much life and body to my hair. Most of all I felt beautiful and confident walking out her door. Judy has been a testitude in the styling industry with her professionalism and passion for healthy hair.

-Marsha Thelusme

## About the Author

I come from a family of 15! Growing up with eight sisters, it was natural for me to love the beauty industry.

I began my journey at Palm Beach Academy of Health and Beauty in 2007 and earned my license in Nail Technology. A year later, with lots of desire and determination, I decided to go to Lincoln College of Technology and became a licensed Cosmetologist in 2008. Working in the industry for a decade now; my passion has flourished into my brand P31 Artistry.

I am passionate about helping women look and feel their best, and that's how P31 Artistry as birthed in 2016. P31 Artistry is committed to servicing women of all ages, not just in beauty and health, but also in ministry. Together we will walk in purpose, fulfilling our dreams, and step into God's Destiny for our lives.

I delight in bringing a vision into reality through Event Design and Consulting. In 2006, I created Alpha & Omega Event Planning. I embraced the gifts and talents that I've been blessed with, and I am passion about supporting other women to do the same in order to support their families and fulfill their dream; thus, becoming a P31 women.

Judy is happily married to Giovanni, and they have a son, Malachi in sunny South Florida.

www.ingramcontent.com/pod-product-compliance
Lightning Source LLC
Chambersburg PA
CBHW071231160426
43196CB00012B/2479